GOD OF COVENANT

A STUDY OF GENESIS 12–50

JEN WILKIN

LifeWay Press® Nashville, Tennessee

EDITORIAL TEAM
ADULT MINISTRY PUBLISHING

Faith Whatley
Director, Adult Ministry

Michelle Hicks
Manager, Adult Ministry
Short Term Bible Studies

Elizabeth Hyndman
Content Editor

Sarah Doss
Production Editor

Heather Wetherington
Art Director

Published by LifeWay Press® • © 2018 Jen Wilkin
Reprinted February 2020

ISBN: 978-1-4627-4889-1

Item: 005794454

Dewey Decimal Classification: 222.11
Subject Headings: BIBLE. O.T. GENESIS / COVENANTS (THEOLOGY) / GOD

Unless otherwise indicated, all Scripture quotations are from The ESV® Bible (The Holy Bible, English Standard Version®), copyright © 2001 by Crossway, a publishing ministry of Good News Publishers. Used by permission. All rights reserved. Scripture quotations marked (NIV) are taken from the Holy Bible, New International Version®, NIV® Copyright © 1973, 1978, 1984, 2011 by Biblica, Inc.™ Used by permission of Zondervan. All rights reserved worldwide. www.zondervan.com. The "NIV" and "New International Version" are trademarks registered in the United States Patent and Trademark Office by Biblica, Inc. ™

To order additional copies of this resource, order online at www.lifeway.com; write LifeWay Christian Resources Customer Service: One LifeWay Plaza, Nashville, TN 37234-0113; fax order to 615.251.5933; or call toll-free 1.800.458.2772.

Printed in the United States of America

Adult Ministry Publishing
LifeWay Resources
One LifeWay Plaza
Nashville, TN 37234

Author is represented by Wolgemuth & Associates.

CONTENTS

ABOUT THE AUTHOR

Jen Wilkin is a wife, mom to four, and an advocate for women to love God with their minds through the faithful study of His Word. She is a speaker, writer, and a teacher of the Bible. Jen lives in Flower Mound, Texas, and her family calls The Village Church home. Jen is the author of *Women of the Word: How to Study the Bible with Both Our Hearts and Our Minds*, *None Like Him: 10 Ways God Is Different From Us (and Why That's a Good Thing)*, *In His Image: 10 Ways God Calls Us to Reflect His Character*, *God of Creation* Bible study, *Sermon on the Mount* Bible study, and *1 Peter: A Living Hope in Christ* Bible study. You can also find her at jenwilkin.net.

FOREWORD: HOW SHOULD WE APPROACH GOD'S WORD?

OUR PURPOSE

The Bible study you are about to begin will teach you an important passage of the Bible in a way that will stay with you for years to come. It will challenge you to move beyond loving God with just your heart to loving Him with your mind. It will focus on answering the question, "What does the Bible say about God?" It will aid you in the worthy task of God-discovery.

You see, the Bible is not a book about self-discovery; it is a book about God-discovery. The Bible is God's declared intent to make Himself known to us. In learning about the character of God in Scripture, we will experience self-discovery, but it must not be the object of our study. The object must be God Himself.

This focus changes the way we study. We look first for what a passage can teach us about the character of God, allowing self-discovery to be the by-product of God-discovery. This is a much better approach because there can be no true knowledge of self apart from knowledge of God. So when I read the account of Jonah, I see first that God is just and faithful to His Word—He is faithful to proclaim His message to Nineveh no matter what. I see second that I, by contrast (and much like Jonah), am unjust to my fellow man and unfaithful to God's Word. Thus, knowledge of God leads to true knowledge of self, which leads to repentance and transformation. So are confirmed Paul's words in Romans 12:2 that we are transformed by the renewing of our minds.

Most of us are good at loving God with our hearts. We are good at employing our emotions in our pursuit of God. But the God who commands us to love with the totality of our hearts, souls, and strength also commands us to love Him with all of our minds. Because He only commands what He also enables His children to do, it must be possible for us to love Him well with our minds or He would not command it. I know you will bring your emotions to your study of God's Word, and that is good and right. But it is your mind that I am jealous for. God intends for you to be a good student, renewing your mind and thus transforming your heart.

OUR PROCESS

Being a good student entails following good study habits. When we sit down to read, most of us like to read through a particular passage and then find a way to apply it to our everyday lives. We may read through an entire book of the Bible over a period of time, or we may jump around from place to place. I want to suggest a different approach, one that may not always yield immediate application, comfort, or peace, but one that builds over time a cumulative understanding of the message of Scripture.

READING IN CONTEXT AND REPETITIVELY

Imagine yourself receiving a letter in the mail. The envelope is handwritten, but you don't glance at the return address. Instead you tear open the envelope, flip to the second page, read two paragraphs near the bottom, and set the letter aside. Knowing that if someone bothered to send it to you, you should act on its contents in some way, you spend a few minutes trying to figure out how to respond to what the section you just read had to say. What are the odds you will be successful?

No one would read a letter this way. But this is precisely the way many of us read our Bibles. We skip past reading the "envelope"—Who wrote this? To whom is it written? When was it written? Where was it written?— and then try to determine the purpose of its contents from a portion of the whole. What if we took time to read the envelope? What if, after determining the context for its writing, we started at the beginning and read to the end? Wouldn't that make infinitely more sense?

In our study, we will take this approach to Scripture. We will begin by placing our text in its historical and cultural context. We will "read the envelope." Then we will read through the entire text multiple times, so that we can better determine what it wants to say to us. We will read repetitively so that we might move through three critical stages of understanding: comprehension, interpretation, and application.

STAGE 1: COMPREHENSION

Remember the reading comprehension section on the SAT? Remember those long reading passages followed by questions to test your knowledge of what you had just read? The objective was to force you to read for detail. We are going to apply the same method to our study of God's Word. When we read for comprehension we ask ourselves, "What does it say?" This is hard work. A person who *comprehends* the account of the six days of creation can tell you specifically what happened on each day. This is the first step toward being able to interpret and apply the story of creation to our lives.

STAGE 2: INTERPRETATION

While comprehension asks, "What does it say?," interpretation asks, "What does it mean?" Once we have read a passage enough times to know what it says, we are ready to look into its meaning. A person who *interprets* the creation story can tell you why God created in a particular order or way. She is able to imply things from the text beyond what it says.

STAGE 3: APPLICATION

After doing the work to understand what the text says and what the text means, we are finally ready to ask, "How should it change me?" Here is where we draw on our God-centered perspective to ask three supporting questions:

- What does this passage teach me about God?
- How does this aspect of God's character change my view of self?
- What should I do in response?

A person who *applies* the creation story can tell us that because God creates in an orderly fashion, we, too, should live well-ordered lives. Knowledge of God gleaned through comprehension of the text and interpretation of its meaning can now be applied to my life in a way that challenges me to be different.

SOME GUIDELINES

It is vital to the learning process that you allow yourself to move through the three stages of understanding on your own, without the aid of commentaries or study notes. The first several times you read a passage, you will probably be confused. This is actually a good thing. Allow yourself to feel lost, to dwell in the "I don't know." It will make the moment of discovery stick.

Nobody likes to feel lost or confused, but it is an important step in the acquisition and retention of understanding. Because of this, I have a few guidelines to lay out for you as you go through this study:

1. **Avoid all commentaries** until *comprehension* and *interpretation* have been earnestly attempted on your own. In other words, wait to read commentaries until after you have done the homework or personal study, attended small-group time, and listened to the teaching. And then, consult commentaries you can trust. Ask a pastor or Bible teacher at your church for suggested authors. A list of commentaries used to create this study can be found on page 191.

2. For the purposes of this study, **get a Bible without study notes.** Come on, it's just too easy to look at them. You know I'm right.

3. Though commentaries are initially off-limits, here are some **tools you should use:**

- **Cross-references.** These are the Scripture references in the margin or at the bottom of the page in your Bible. They point you to other passages that deal with the same topic or theme.

- **An English dictionary** to look up unfamiliar words.

- **Other translations of the Bible.** We will use the English Standard Version (ESV) as a starting point, but you can easily consult other versions online. I recommend the Christian Standard Version (CSB), New International Version (NIV), New American Standard Version (NASB), or the New King James Version (NKJV). Reading more than one translation can expand your understanding of the meaning of a passage. Note: a paraphrase, such as The Message, can be useful but should be regarded as a commentary rather than a translation. They are best consulted after careful study of an actual translation.

- **A printed copy of the text,** double-spaced, so you can mark repeated words, phrases, or ideas.

STORING UP TREASURE

Approaching God's Word with a God-centered perspective, with context, and with care takes effort and commitment. It is study for the long-term. Some days your study may not move you emotionally or speak to an immediate need. You may not be able to apply a passage at all. But what if ten years from now, in a dark night of the soul, that passage suddenly opens up to you because of the work you have done today? Wouldn't your long-term investment be worth it?

In Matthew 13, we see Jesus begin to teach in parables. He tells seven deceptively simple stories that leave His disciples struggling for understanding—dwelling in the "I don't know," if you will. After the last parable, He turns to them and asks, "Have you understood all these things?" (v. 51). Despite their apparent confusion, they answer out of their earnest desire with, "Yes" (v. 51). Jesus tells them that their newfound understanding makes them "like the owner of a house who brings out of his storeroom new treasures as well as old" (13:52, NIV).

A storeroom, as Jesus indicates, is a place for keeping valuables over a long period of time for use when needed. Faithful study of God's Word is a means for filling our spiritual storerooms with truth, so that in our hour of need we can bring forth both the old and the new as a source of rich provision. I pray that this study would be for you a source of much treasure and that you would labor well to obtain it.

Grace and peace,

Jen Wilkin

HOW TO USE THIS STUDY

This Bible study book is designed to be used in a specific way. The homework in the Bible study book will start you in the process of comprehension, interpretation, and application. However, it was designed to dovetail with small-group discussion time and the teaching sessions. You can use the Bible study book by itself, but you are likely to find yourself with some unresolved questions. The teaching sessions are intended to resolve most, if not all, of your unanswered questions from the homework and discussion time. With this in mind, consider using the materials as follows:

- If you are going through the study **on your own**, first work through the homework, and then watch or listen to the corresponding teaching for that week.

- If you are going through the study **in a group**, first do your homework, and then discuss the questions your group decides to cover. Then watch or listen to the teaching. Some groups watch or listen to the teaching before they meet, which can also work if that format fits best for everyone.

Note: For Week One, there is no homework. The study begins with an audio or video introduction. You will find a Viewer Guide on pages 14-15 that you can use as you watch or listen to the introductory material.

HOW TO USE THE LEADER GUIDE

At the end of each week's personal study you will find a leader guide intended to help facilitate discussion in small groups. Each guide begins with an introductory question to help group members get to know each other and feel comfortable contributing their voices to the discussion.

These questions may prove to be most helpful during the early weeks of the study, but as the group grows more familiar with one another, group leaders may decide to skip them to allow more time for the questions covering the lesson.

The remainder of the leader guide includes questions to help group members compare what they have learned from their personal study on Days Two through Five. These questions are either pulled directly from the personal study, or they summarize a concept or theme that the personal study covered. Each two-part question covers content from a particular day of the personal study, first asking group members to reflect and then asking them to apply. The reflection questions typically ask group members to report a finding or flesh out an interpretation. The application questions challenge them to move beyond intellectual understanding and to identify ways to live differently in light of what they have learned.

As a small group leader, you will want to review these questions before you meet with your group, thinking through your own answers, marking where they occur in the personal study, and noting if there are any additional questions that you might want to reference to help the flow of the discussion. These questions are suggestions only, intended to help you cover as much ground as you can in a 45-minute discussion time. They should not be seen as requirements or limitations, but as guidelines to help you prepare your group for the teaching time by allowing them to process collectively what they have learned during their personal study.

As a facilitator of discussion rather than a teacher, you are allowed and encouraged to be a co-learner with your group members. This means you yourself may not always feel confident of your answer to a given question, and that is perfectly OK. Because we are studying for the long-term, we are allowed to leave some questions partially answered or unresolved, trusting for clarity at a later time. In most cases, the teaching time should address any lingering questions that are not resolved in the personal study or the small-group discussion time.

WEEK ONE:
GENESIS INTRODUCTION

Who wrote the Book of Genesis?

Moses

When was it written?

between 1600 - 1400 B.C.
3500 years ago

To whom was it written?

Isrealities

In what style was it written?

historical narrative

What is the central theme of the book?

A begining

CALLING AND COVENANT

In Genesis 12–50 we see God give and begin to fulfill the covenant promise that His people will be numerous, will have a land of their own, and will be a source of blessing to the whole world. Over the next ten weeks we will watch that promise begin to unfold through the lives of four generations of men: Abraham, Isaac, Jacob, and Joseph. If you have ever wondered about the origin of the twelve tribes of Israel or how they came to be enslaved in Egypt, Genesis 12–50 will help you (as it helped its original audience) trace the events and the family trees that shape the history recorded in Exodus and beyond. But it all starts with a man named Abram, a Mesopotamian city dweller whom God uproots for His sovereign purpose.

This week, we will meet Abram—a man of faith and a man of flaws—as he journeys from Ur to Canaan, to Egypt, and back to Canaan. We will be introduced to Sarai, Abram's wife, who displays a willingness to help her husband hedge his bets, even at great personal cost. We also get a first glimpse into Lot's willingness to place himself in close proximity to wickedness. And we meet Melchizedek: king of peace, priest of God Most High, bearer of bread and wine. We will watch as Abram learns about God's plans for him and for his descendants. We'll see the patience of God try the patience of man, and we'll explore how to live in light of God's unshakeable promises.

Note: Each week we will cover between three and six chapters of text. Because of this, at the beginning of each week's lesson, you will be asked to summarize each chapter into one to two sentences. Though it may seem like a monotonous task, summarizing is a powerful skill for the earnest student of God's Word. Don't hurry past this opportunity to practice it. By the end of the study, you will have created a summary overview of Genesis 12–50 in your own words.

DAY ONE
READ THROUGH GENESIS 12–16 FROM START TO FINISH.

1. Summarize each chapter in one to two sentences. (You can copy your
    chapter summaries onto the summary sheets in the appendix of your
    Bible study book to build a complete overview of the text. See p. 184.)
    CHAPTER 12

    CHAPTER 13

    CHAPTER 14

    CHAPTER 15

    CHAPTER 16

2. Below is a map of Abram's route. Read through 12:4-9, and note on
    the map each place Abram builds an altar. (Note: Bethel was located
    between Shechem and Jerusalem.)

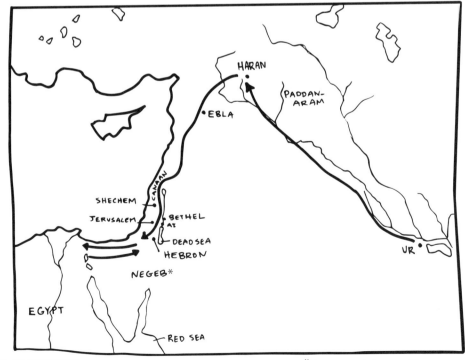

HARAN

PADDAN-ARAM

•EBLA

CANAAN

SHECHEM

JERUSALEM

•BETHEL
AI

DEAD SEA
HEBRON

NEGEB*

UR •

EGYPT

RED SEA

* Some translations say Negev.

NOW LOOK MORE CLOSELY AT GENESIS 12–13.

3. In 12:1, what three things is Abram told to *go from*?

    1.

    2.

    3.

    What is Abram told to *go to*?

    If you were Abram, how would you likely feel about this destination?

4. In 12:1-3, we have our first glimpse of the future God has planned for
    Abram. Notice the repetition of the words "I will." Below, note each of
    the five things God tells Abram "[He] will" do in 12:1-3.

    1. "I will ... _____ "
    2. "I will ... _____ "
    3. "I will ... _____ "
    4. "I will ... _____ "
    5. "I will ... _____ "

5. What do we learn about Abram's character in 12:4-9? Read through these six verses and note below what you find. (You may want to peek at Hebrews 11:8-10 to help you get started.)

CHARACTER TRAITS	HOW ABRAM DEMONSTRATES THEM

6. Now look at 12:10-20. Why does Abram take his family to Egypt?

Does Abram lie to Pharaoh about Sarai? Look ahead to Genesis 20:12 to help with your answer.

Though Sarai is silent during this part of the story, what might have been her thoughts and feelings about Abram's survival plan?

7. Did Abram's actions in Egypt threaten God's plan to make him a great nation? Explain your answer.

8. On the map on page 18, note where Abram journeys in chapter 13.

9. What problem did Abram and Lot have (13:5-7)? How did Abram resolve the problem (13:8-9)?

    Where did Lot choose to settle (13:12)? How does his choice contrast to Abram's choice of land?

10. Mark the city of Sodom on your map around the southernmost tip of the Dead Sea.

11. **APPLY:** In 13:14-18, God reiterates His promise to Abram.

    What significant two words are repeated once again in this passage?

    Why are those repeated words significant to Abram then?

    To us, as the church, now?

DAY THREE
NOW LOOK AT GENESIS 14.

12. In Canaan, a king would have been the ruler of a walled city. He was also often the high priest of the god of that particular city. In the chart below, note the kings who battled against each other (14:1-2).

Amraphel, king of _____	Bera, king of _____

13. What tactic did Abram use to defeat Chedorlaomer's forces? What does that tell you about Abram?

14. Apparently what did a conquering king typically acquire when he defeated an enemy (14:16)?

15. Melchizedek is an intriguing figure in the Bible. The author of Hebrews tells us that he prefigures Christ, that he gives us a picture of what Christ would be like (Heb. 7). We will discuss him more in our time together, but for now, what details about Melchizedek in 14:17-24 seem to point to Christ?

16. What does Abram's response to the king of Sodom's offer of the spoils tell you about his character?

17. In these first three chapters of the story of Abram, how has God already demonstrated to Abram that, despite all obstacles (including Abram's unrighteousness), "He will" fulfill what He has promised?

18. **APPLY:** Think of a time you were offered something of value your conscience would not allow you to accept. What wrong thinking makes us hesitate before turning away when faced with an offer we know does not honor the Lord? What does Abram's example teach us about the value of a clean conscience?

NOW LOOK AT GENESIS 15.

19. Compare 15:1 in the ESV and the NIV. What understanding do you gain about Abram's reward?

How do God's words to Abram make sense within the context of what has just happened in the previous chapter? Specifically, why would God reassure Abram that *He Himself* was:

ABRAM'S SHIELD

ABRAM'S GREAT REWARD

20. What does Abram's reply in 15:2-3 indicate his greatest fear to be?

Is his fear unreasonable? See 11:30 and 12:4. (Note that some time has passed since 12:4.) What factors are contributing to his fear?

21. Genesis 15:6 is one of the most frequently quoted Old Testament verses by New Testament authors. Write the verse below, using "God" and "Abram" in place of the personal pronouns:

Why do you think this verse is so often quoted? (You may want to find a few places it is used in the New Testament to help with your answer).

God formalizes His promises to Abram in a ceremony that would have been easily recognizable to the people of Moses' time. It was a covenant, their version of signing legally-binding contracts at a time when those kinds of documents were not used. The concept of covenant is central to our understanding of God and of our salvation. In the Bible, God enters into a number of covenants with man. In Genesis 1–11, we have already seen an implied covenant between God and Adam (2:15-17) and a spoken covenant between God and Noah (8:21-22; 9:8-11). Now we come to the third covenant between God and man—the Abrahamic covenant.

22. Look back at 12:2-3,6-7. Then use the additional information you find in chapter 15 to answer the questions below.

	ABRAHAMIC COVENANT
Who initiates the covenant?	
What two parties are involved in the covenant?	
What does God promise? (12:1,6-7; 15:18-21)	1.
(12:2; 15:4-5)	2.
(12:3; 15:14-16)	3.
What is required of Abraham?	
What is the penalty for breach of the covenant?	

23. What do you think the smoking fire pot and flaming torch represent in 15:17?

24. **APPLY:** How have you known God to be your shield? Your great reward? Write a specific example of each below.

NOW LOOK AT GENESIS 16.

25. At this point in the story, Abram is eighty-five years old and Sarai is around seventy-five. Ten years have passed between the first promise of an heir and Sarai's scheme with Hagar.

    When God promised an heir to Abram in 12:2, what key detail did He leave out? Why do you think this is the case?

26. What do Sarai's actions in chapter 16 reveal about what she believes about God? About herself?

27. In 16:4-6, who behaves badly? List your prime suspects and theories below.

28. In 16:7-16, what do you learn about the character of God from His treatment of Hagar? List some thoughts below.

29. Think of all the things God named in Genesis 1: day, night, earth, heaven, the seas, man. How is God's naming of Ishmael different from Hagar's naming of God?

30. **APPLY:** When have you behaved like Sarai, allowing fear or self-reliance to govern your actions? How did your plans turn out?

When have you behaved like Abram, deferring to human wisdom over God's will? What was the outcome?

WRAP-UP

What aspect of God's character has this week's passage of Genesis shown you more clearly?

Fill in the following statement:
Knowing that God is _____ shows me that I am
_____.

What one step can you take this week to better live in light of this truth?

INTRODUCTORY QUESTION: When did you last move? How did you feel about the move before it took place? After?

1. OBSERVE: (question 7, p. 21) Did Abram's actions in Egypt threaten God's plan to make him a great nation? Explain your answer.

APPLY: (question 11, p. 21) In 13:14-18, God reiterates His promise to Abram. What significant two words are repeated once again in this passage?

Why are those repeated words significant to Abram then? To us, as the church, now?

2. OBSERVE: (question 16, p. 23) What does Abram's response to the king of Sodom's offer of the spoils tell you about his character?

APPLY: (question 18, p. 23) Think of a time you were offered something of value your conscience would not allow you to accept. What wrong thinking makes us hesitate before turning away when faced with an offer we know does not honor the Lord? What does Abram's example teach us about the value of a clean conscience?

3. OBSERVE: (question 19, p. 24) How do God's words to Abram make sense within the context of what has just happened in the previous chapter? Specifically, why would God reassure Abram that *He Himself* was:

ABRAM'S SHIELD
ABRAM'S GREAT REWARD

APPLY: (question 24, p. 26) How have you known God to be your shield? Your great reward?

4. OBSERVE: (question 27, p. 27) In 16:4-6, who behaves badly?

APPLY: (question 30, p. 28) When have you behaved like Sarai, allowing fear or self-reliance to govern your actions? How did your plans turn out?

When have you behaved like Abram, deferring to human wisdom over God's will? What was the outcome?

5. **WRAP-UP:** What aspect of God's character has this week's passage of Genesis shown you more clearly?

Fill in the following statement:
Knowing that God is _____ shows me that I am
_____.

What one step can you take this week to better live in light of this truth?

WEEK TWO | VIEWER GUIDE NOTES

Teaching sessions available
for purchase or rent at
LifeWay.com/GodOfCovenant

WEEK TWO: CALLING AND COVENANT   33

WEEK THREE:

GOD VISITS

Last week we witnessed the intent of a covenant-making God to create a people for Himself from which the Savior of the whole world would come. But He would do it on His own time. We watched our spiritual parents grow impatient, trying to take matters into their own hands to produce an heir.

This week we'll see the institution of God's covenant sign and His renewal of the promise of an heir to a newly named Abraham. And we'll gain further insight into the character of the man called the "friend of God" and the woman who would give birth to a nation. We'll learn, with Abraham, about God's justice and mercy as the smoke rises over Sodom, and we'll watch both Abraham and Sarah struggle with the answer to the question, "Is anything too hard for the LORD?" (Gen. 18:14).

READ GENESIS 17–20 FROM START TO FINISH, AND THEN ANSWER THE QUESTIONS BELOW.

1. Summarize each chapter in one to two sentences. (You can copy your chapter summaries onto the summary sheets in the appendix of the workbook to build a complete overview of the text. See p. 184.)

   CHAPTER 17

   CHAPTER 18

   CHAPTER 19

   CHAPTER 20

2. What new insights do you gain about the strengths and weaknesses of:

   ABRAHAM:

   SARAH:

   LOT:

DAY TWO
NOW LOOK AT GENESIS 17.

3. For whom does God choose a new name? (17:5,15) _____

    What do the new names mean? (Check the footnotes in your Bible.)

    Why do you think God gives these new names?

4. Most covenants were accompanied by a sign. What was to be the sign
    of God's covenant with Abram/Abraham (17:11)?

    Why do you think God chose this as the sign of His covenant?

5. In 17:6-8, what significant phrase is repeated? _____

    How is it significant? How does it reinforce your answer to question 4
    above?

6. Look at 17:15-27. What emotion do you think Abraham is expressing by
    his reaction in 17:17?

    What emotion is indicated by his words in 17:18?

7. What important new details does God share with Abraham (17:19,21)?
THE CHILD'S NAME:

THE TIME OF HIS ARRIVAL:

8. **APPLY:** Abraham placed his faith in the God of "I will," and it was credited to him as righteousness. You and I place our faith in the God of "It is finished." They are the same God, viewed through two different angles of human perspective. How does our New Covenant perspective help us trust that "he who began a good work in [us] will bring it to completion" (Phil. 1:6)?

DAY THREE

NOW LOOK AT GENESIS 18:1-15.

9. Who are the three men who visit Abraham? Glance forward to 19:1, and write below who each is, according to what you can tell from the text.

   1.

   2.

   3.

   Do you think Abraham immediately recognizes who his visitors are (18:2)?

10. Compare what Abraham says he will do for his visitors to what he actually does.

WHAT HE SAYS (18:4-5)	WHAT HE DOES (18:6-8)

   What do you think explains the difference between his words and his actions? What does it reveal about his character? List some thoughts below.

11. What does 18:11 want us to know about Sarah?

    What key question does Sarah need to come to terms with (18:14)?

12. Look back at 17:15-17. Why do you think God rebukes Sarah for laughing but not Abraham?

13. Look at 18:15. What does Sarah's lie demonstrate she believes about God?

    What does God's response demonstrate? (Compare to two other famous falsifiers in Acts 5:1-11.)

14. **APPLY:** What circumstance has caused you to face the question, "Is anything too hard for the LORD?" Why are we often tempted to answer this question with "Yes"? How has God shown Himself faithful, either in your waiting or in the resolution of your difficulty?

DAY FOUR
NOW FOCUS ON GENESIS 18:16-33.

15. Why do you think God shares His plan to destroy Sodom with Abraham?

16. How do you reconcile the statement in 18:20-21 with the truth that God knows all things?

17. What do we learn about the character of Abraham in 18:23-33? List some thoughts and your reasoning below.

   What do we learn in this passage about the character of God? List some thoughts and your reasoning below.

18. Does Abraham change God's mind or actions? Explain your answer.

NOW LOOK AT GENESIS 19:1-29.

19. Why do you think the two men (angels) first refuse Lot's offer of hospitality? Why does Lot "[press] them strongly" (v. 3)?

20. In 19:4-5, what is the intent of the men who surround the house?

21. In 19:6-8 what do we learn about Lot's character from his response to the men? Note your thoughts below:

WHAT LOT SAYS	WHAT LOT REVEALS ABOUT HIMSELF
"I beg you, my brothers ..."	
" ... do not act so wickedly."	
"Behold, I have two daughters who have not known any man. Let me bring them out to you, and do to them as you please."	
"Only do nothing to these men, for they have come under the shelter of my roof."	

22. How many righteous people were found in Sodom (19:15)? _____

What does 19:16 teach us about Lot? About God?

23. What does Lot do in 19:18-20? Check your answer below:

    _____ Repents of his foolishness
    _____ Agrees to do exactly as he is told
    _____ Bargains for a more favorable place to flee

How is Lot's request different than Abraham's request in the previous chapter (18:22-32)?

24. Why do you think God turned Lot's wife into a pillar of salt, instead of some other substance (19:26)?

25. In 19:27-28, what do you think Abraham was thinking as he looked down toward Sodom?

26. **APPLY:** How have you known the faithfulness of God to deliver you from self-inflicted hardship due to foolish choices?

NOW LOOK AT GENESIS 19:30–20:18.

Just when you thought things couldn't get worse.

27. What do Lot's two virgin daughters decide to do (19:30-38)? Why?

    What does their behavior and their declared intent (19:32,34) indicate they believe to be true about their value as women?

28. Chapter 20 brings us back to a familiar storyline. Oh the burden of having a smokin' hot octogenarian wife. Or maybe we should say "Oh, the benefit?" In the space below, note any similarities or differences between the story of Abram in Egypt (12:1-20) and the story of Abraham and Abimelech.

SIMILARITIES	DIFFERENCES

29. How is this story of Abraham and Abimelech a cautionary tale for us? Is the story reassuring in any way?

30. What do we learn about cultural attitudes toward women (their roles, value, identity, etc.) based on the following:

TREATMENT	UNDERLYING ATTITUDE TOWARD WOMEN
Sarai is given to Pharaoh.	
Hagar is sent in to Abram.	
Hagar's disdain for Sarai.	
Sarai's disdain for Hagar.	
Lot raises two virgins in Sodom.	
Lot offers his virgin daughters to the mob.	
Lot's daughters commit incest to secure offspring.	
Sarah is given to Abimelech.	

Which of these attitudes toward women persist in our culture today? Note them above with an "X."

31. **APPLY:** Note that in the chart above, men were not the only ones buying into wrong cultural attitudes about women. How do both modern men and women give assent to similar attitudes in the way they think, speak, or act? Give three specific examples below.

1.

2.

3.

How does the gospel reject these wrong views of women? How does it grant them dignity and worth?

WRAP-UP

What aspect of God's character has this week's passage of Genesis shown you more clearly?

Fill in the following statement:

Knowing that God is _____ shows me that I am _____.

What one step can you take this week to better live in light of this truth?

INTRODUCTORY QUESTION: Do you know why your name was chosen for you? What does your name mean?

1. OBSERVE: (question 5, p. 37) In 17:6-8, what significant phrase is repeated?

How is it significant? How does it reinforce your answer to the previous question?

APPLY: (question 8, p. 38) Abraham placed his faith in the God of "I will," and it was credited to him as righteousness. You and I place our faith in the God of "It is finished." They are the same God, viewed through two different angles of human perspective. How does our New Covenant perspective help us trust that "he who began a good work in [us] will bring it to completion" (Phil 1:6)?

2. OBSERVE: (question 13, p. 40) Look at 18:15. What does Sarah's lie demonstrate she believes about God?

What does God's response demonstrate? (Compare Acts 5:1-11.)

APPLY: (question 14, p. 40) What circumstance has caused you to face the question, "Is anything too hard for the Lord?" Why are we often tempted to answer this question with "Yes"? How has God shown Himself faithful, either in your waiting or in the resolution of your difficulty?

3. OBSERVE: (question 22, p. 42) How many righteous people were found in Sodom (19:15)? _____

What does 19:16 teach us about Lot? About God?

APPLY: (question 26, p. 43) How have you known the faithfulness of God to deliver you from self-inflicted hardship due to foolish choices?

4. **OBSERVE:** (question 30, p. 45) Which of the negative cultural attitudes toward women that you noted persist in our culture today?

APPLY: (question 31, p. 45-46) Note that men were not the only ones buying into wrong cultural attitudes about women. How do both modern men and women give assent to similar attitudes in the way they think, speak, or act?

How does the gospel reject these wrong views of women? How does it grant them dignity and worth?

5. **WRAP-UP:** What aspect of God's character has this week's passage of Genesis shown you more clearly?

Fill in the following statement:

Knowing that God is _____ shows me that I am
_____.

What one step can you take this week to better live in light of this truth?

WEEK THREE | VIEWER GUIDE NOTES

_____

_____

_____

_____

_____

_____

_____

_____

_____

_____

_____

_____

_____

_____

_____

_____

_____

_____

_____

_____

_____

_____

Teaching sessions available
for purchase or rent at
LifeWay.com/GodOfCovenant

WEEK THREE: GOD VISITS   51

WEEK FOUR:

THE LONG-AWAITED SON

At long last, Isaac arrives—a miraculous birth that emphatically answers the question "Is anything too hard for the LORD?"

If Abraham's life were made into a movie, the director would probably be tempted to roll the credits and drop the curtain right after the birth of the child. But the story is far from over. This week we will learn how Abraham secured his name in history as the "man of faith." We'll watch him bury his wife, attach himself to the land of promise, make provision for his son, and go to his rest. And as the curtain falls on the life of this great man, we will turn our eyes to the fulfillment of God's promise through Isaac—the child born of God's will.

READ GENESIS 21–25:18 FROM START TO FINISH, AND THEN ANSWER THE QUESTIONS BELOW.

1. Summarize each chapter in one to two sentences:

    CHAPTER 21

    CHAPTER 22

    CHAPTER 23

    CHAPTER 24

    CHAPTER 25:1-18

NOW LOOK BACK AT 21:1-21.

2. In 21:1-2, who is faithful to whom?

    In 21:3-4, who is faithful to whom?

3. In 21:6-7, how is Sarah's laughter different than her previous laughter episode in 18:12?

4. Read 21:9 in the ESV and NIV. What action of Ishmael's angers Sarah?

    What do you think of her reaction (21:10)? Does it seem just? Why or why not?

    How did Abraham feel about her reaction (21:11)?

5. What do you think about God's response to Abraham in 21:12-13? Does it seem just? Why or why not?

6. How do we see Abraham behaving in 21:14? (How does the fact that he "rose early in the morning" shape your answer?)

7. How is Hagar's story in 21:15-21 similar to the last time we saw her in the wilderness (16:6-14)? List similarities below.

8. Now read Galatians 4:21-31. Even though Sarah acts out of anger toward Hagar, how was Hagar's expulsion a part of God's plan and a picture of our redemption? List your thoughts below.

   Mount Sinai is where Moses was given the law. From what slavery have the children of the promise been freed (Gal. 4:21,25)?

9. **APPLY:** As a believer, you are the spiritual "child of the free woman." In what ways are you prone to live forgetfully as the "child of the slave woman," in bondage to the law? How are you most likely to try to earn God's favor?

DAY THREE
NOW LOOK AT 21:22-34.

10. In this passage, we gain some insight into the relationship between two great leaders: one who is a native and one who is an outsider.
WHO IS THE NATIVE?

WHO IS THE OUTSIDER?

11. Why do you think Abimelech wanted peaceful relations with Abraham?

12. How would you describe the tone of relations between the two men?

_____ Hostile
_____ Mutually Respectful
_____ Affectionate

13. How much do you think the two men have in common in the following areas?
RELIGION:

POLITICS:

DESIRE FOR PEACE AND JUSTICE:

14. Read Romans 13:1-7. How are the authorities referred to in 13:6?

    What does 13:7 tell us is due to these authorities?

    _____ _____ _____ _____

15. **APPLY:** Abraham's dealings with Abimelech demonstrate that he understood the concept outlined in Romans 13. Do you think Christians living in the United States today demonstrate an understanding of this concept? Why or why not?

DAY FOUR
NOW LOOK AT GENESIS 22.

16. What does Abraham's response to the call of God in 22:1 indicate?

    Who else in Scripture responds to the call of God like this? List any that come to mind.

17. In 22:2 look at how God describes Isaac to Abraham: "your son, your only son … whom you love." How is this a significant statement? Look up the following verses, and note what you find:
    MATTHEW 3:17

    MATTHEW 17:5

    JOHN 3:16

    EPHESIANS 1:5-6

    2 PETER 1:17

18. Where was Isaac to be sacrificed (22:2)?

    What future significance would this location hold? Look up
    2 Chronicles 3:1.

19. What does Genesis 22:3 tell you about the character of Abraham?

20. How many days does the trip take (22:4)? _____
    What do you think these days were like for Abraham?

21. In 22:5-8, what does Abraham seem to believe will be the outcome of
    this terrible situation? Note where you find your clues. Then look up
    Hebrews 11:19 to confirm your answer.

22. In Genesis 22:6-14, what shadows of the story of Christ do you see?
    Note as many as you can find below.

23. In 22:11-12, does God learn anything about Abraham that He didn't already know?

Why do you think God tested Abraham?

24. **APPLY:** Have you ever had your faith put to the test, perhaps not as dramatically as Abraham, in a way that marked you? How did it change you?

NOW LOOK AT GENESIS 23.

25. It was customary for a family to bury their dead in the place of their ancestors. How is it significant that Abraham decides to bury Sarah in the place of his sojourning?

26. Abraham, an outsider, negotiates with Ephron the son of Zohar in the presence of the Hittite leaders to purchase a cave. How is he regarded among these leaders (23:6)?

27. Skim through 23:10-20. Based on knowledge of real estate values in Abraham's day from historical sources (including the Bible), many commentators believe that Ephron's asking price was well above the value of the cave.[1] What does it say about Abraham that he paid Ephron's asking price?

28. Write an epitaph for Sarah. What would her headstone say, if she had had one?
    HERE LIES SARAH,

NOW LOOK AT GENESIS 24.

29. Where does Abraham send his servant to get a wife for Isaac (24:1-4)? Why?

   Why do you think he is adamant that Isaac not go there, but that the servant go instead (24:5-9)?

30. How many camels did the servant have with him (24:10)? _____

   A thirsty camel may drink about 15-25 gallons of water in one watering.[2] How much water would need to be drawn for the camels? _____ gallons How does this give insight into why the servant chose the test he did?

31. What is Rebekah's relationship to Abraham? She is his

   _____ (24:15).

NOW LOOK AT GENESIS 25.

32. What interesting facts about Abraham do we learn in the following verses?
   25:1 (SEE 1 CHRONICLES 1:32 FOR FURTHER CLARIFICATION.)

   25:5

25:6

25:7

33. What are we reminded of at the end of Ishmael's genealogy (25:18)?

34. What epitaph would you write for Abraham?
   HERE LIES ABRAHAM,

35. What epitaph did others in Scripture give Abraham?
   ISAIAH 41:8-9

   JOHN 8:56

   ROMANS 4:18

   GALATIANS 3:6-9

HEBREWS 6:15

JAMES 2:21-23

36. **APPLY:** Which of the statements above strikes you personally as a desirable epitaph? What do you hope will be said about you when you are gone?

WRAP-UP

What aspect of God's character has this week's passage of Genesis shown you more clearly?

Fill in the following statement:
Knowing that God is _____ shows me that I am _____.

What one step can you take this week to better live in light of this truth?

INTRODUCTORY QUESTION: Would you rather vacation in a city or in a remote countryside? Why?

1. **OBSERVE:** (question 8, p. 56) Read Galatians 4:21-31. Even though Sarah acts out of anger towards Hagar, how was Hagar's expulsion a part of God's plan and a picture of our redemption?

   Mount Sinai is where Moses was given the law. From what slavery have the children of the promise been freed (Gal. 4:21,25)?

   APPLY: (question 9, p. 56) As a believer, you are the spiritual "child of the free woman." In what ways are you prone to live forgetfully as the "child of the slave woman," in bondage to the law? How are you most likely to try to earn God's favor?

2. **OBSERVE:** (question 14, p. 58) Read Romans 13:1-7. How are the authorities referred to in 13:6?

   What does 13:7 tell us is due to these authorities?

   APPLY: (question 15, p. 58) Abraham's dealings with Abimelech demonstrate that he understood the concept outlined in Romans 13. Do you think Christians living in the United States today demonstrate an understanding of this concept? Why or why not?

3. **OBSERVE:** (question 23, p. 61) In 22:11-12, does God learn anything about Abraham that He didn't already know?

   Why do you think God tested Abraham?

   APPLY: (question 24, p. 61) Have you ever had your faith put to the test, perhaps not as dramatically as Abraham, in a way that marked you? How did it change you?

4. **OBSERVE:** (question 34, p. 64) What epitaph would you write for Abraham?

APPLY: (question 36, p. 65) Which of the statements in Scripture about Abraham strikes you personally as a desirable epitaph? What do you hope will be said about you when you are gone?

5. **WRAP-UP:** What aspect of God's character has this week's passage of Genesis shown you more clearly?

Fill in the following statement:

Knowing that God is _____ shows me that I am
_____.

What one step can you take this week to better live in light of this truth?

Teaching sessions available
for purchase or rent at
LifeWay.com/GodOfCovenant

WEEK FOUR: THE LONG-AWAITED SON   69

WEEK FIVE:

SIBLING RIVALRY

Abraham and Sarah have gone to their rest, and the scene shifts to Isaac and his offspring. Isaac and Rebekah raise a family like many families—one full of friction and favoritism. This week we will be introduced to one of the most famous sibling rivalries of all time—that of Jacob and Esau, the twins who begin their struggle for supremacy even before they emerge from the womb. And we'll confront again the truth that God's chosen servants are fragmented and flawed, that we might know our salvation "depends not on human will or exertion, but on God, who has mercy" (Rom. 9:16).

**READ GENESIS 25:19–28:22 FROM START TO FINISH,
AND THEN ANSWER THE QUESTIONS BELOW.**

1. Summarize each chapter in one to two sentences:

   CHAPTER 25:19-34

   CHAPTER 26

   CHAPTER 27

   CHAPTER 28

2. Look at the opening phrase of 25:19. Whose story does it signal the beginning of?

DAY TWO
NOW LOOK AT GENESIS 25:19-34.

3. How old was Isaac when he married Rebekah (25:20)?

    _____

    How long did Isaac and Rebekah wait for a child (25:26)?

    _____

4. How was Isaac's response to the test of barrenness different than that of his parents?

    Why do you think God allowed barrenness for both Abraham and Isaac?

5. What prophecy does God give to Rebekah regarding her sons (25:23)?

6. What color is associated with the name Esau? _____

    What does the name Jacob mean? _____

7. Describe the family dynamics in Isaac's household (25:27-28). What do you think of Isaac and Rebekah's approach to parenting?

8. In 25:30, a more literal translation of Esau's request for stew would be "Gimme some of the red stuff—that red stuff."[1] What is your impression of Esau in this section? What modern-day stereotype would describe him?

9. Look up the following verses and note what they teach about Esau's character:
    PHILIPPIANS 3:18-19

    HEBREWS 12:16-17

10. Look up the word *birthright* in a dictionary. Write a definition for it below that best fits the way it is used in the text.
    BIRTHRIGHT:

11. The birthright of the firstborn son entitled Esau to a double portion of the inheritance as well as leadership of the family after his father's death.[2] What do you think is meant by the statement, "Thus Esau despised his birthright" (25:34)?

12. Esau's birthright entitled him to great material wealth. What other aspect of his birthright did he "despise" when he sold it to Jacob? Look at 12:2-3.

13. **APPLY:** When have you been tempted to give up a long-term gift from God for something that would bring immediate pleasure? Think of an example from your own life.

How does Esau's story encourage you to resist the temptation to sacrifice the permanent on the altar of the temporary?

NOW LOOK AT GENESIS 26.

14. Why do you think God inspired Moses to include this particular incident from Isaac's life in the narrative?

15. This is probably the same Abimelech from Genesis 20.[3] What do you think Abimelech thinks of Abraham's son?

16. Note the similarities in what followed the test of famine for Isaac and for Abraham. Both experienced material blessing, strife, and separation. Fill in the chart below to note the contrast:

	ABRAHAM (13:1-9)	ISAAC (26:12-16)
Material blessing in the form of ...		
Strife with ...		
Separation from ...		

17. Remember the pact between Abimelech and Abraham regarding wells (21:22-34)? What does the fact that the Philistines plugged up Abraham's wells tell you about:

THEIR RESPECT FOR ABRAHAM?

THEIR FEAR OF ABRAHAM'S GOD?

18. Why do the Philistines make a pact with Isaac (26:28-29)?

19. What significant fact(s) do we learn about Esau in 26:34-35?

20. **APPLY:** Isaac follows the example of his father Abraham, repeating his sin. Who looks to you as a spiritual parent?

How can you model godliness for the person you noted, both in the way you obey and in the way you handle your own mistakes?

NOW LOOK AT CHAPTER 27.

21. If he already has the birthright, why does Jacob now also want the blessing? What do you think is the difference between the two things?

22. What senses does Isaac rely on in bestowing his blessing?
    27:22

    27:25

    27:27

23. What emotion do you think the narrator intends us to feel toward Esau when he discovers the blessing has been given to Jacob (27:30-38)? Explain your answer.

24. At the end of the chapter, what is Esau's plan for his brother (27:41)?

What is Rebekah's solution (27:43-44)?

25. We can assume Rebekah would have told Isaac that God intends the blessing to be given to Jacob (Gen. 25:23). Isaac determines to bless Esau despite most likely knowing that information. Read Galatians 6:7. How did Isaac learn the truth of this verse with regard to:
PRACTICING DECEPTION? (REMEMBER GENESIS 26:7.)

PRACTICING FAVORITISM?

26. **APPLY:** How have you learned the truth of Galatians 6:7 in your own life? What seeds of deception or favoritism have yielded a hard harvest within your primary relationships? How have you worked (or how might you work) to sow peace into those relationships?

NOW LOOK AT CHAPTER 28.

27. In 28:1-5, compare Isaac's plan for getting a wife for his son to that of Abraham (24:1-9). What is similar? What is different? Fill in the chart below. Note any reasons that might account for differences.

SIMILARITIES	DIFFERENCES

28. What factors prompt Esau's decision to marry a third time (28:6-9)?

How do you think Esau's choice of Mahalath may be an attempt to regain his father's approval?

Mahalath is the daughter of _____, the granddaughter of _____.

How does Esau's choice show a continuing lack of spiritual understanding?

29. In 28:10-22, we see Jacob begin his journey toward Haran to find a wife in the house of his Uncle Laban. On the map below, highlight how far Jacob had traveled by the time he has his vision.

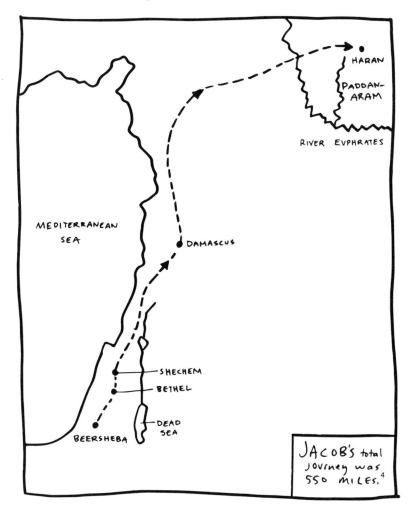

How does the total length of the journey shape your understanding of why Abraham sent a servant to get Rebekah instead of sending Isaac himself?

30. In the space below, draw a picture of what Jacob saw in his vision (28:12-17). Read the account in the ESV and NIV before you start drawing.

31. What is Jacob's reaction to/interpretation of what he has seen (28:16-17)?
    REACTION:

    INTERPRETATION:

32. Thankfully, we are not left to wonder what this strange dream signifies. In John 1, in response to Nathanael's recognition of who He is, Jesus tells Nathanael that he will see far greater truths about Jesus than he has yet discovered. Read John 1:51 to see how Jesus describes what Nathanael will witness. Write what you find below.

    What do you think Jesus means? Look at the following verses to help you answer:
    JOHN 14:6

    1 TIMOTHY 2:5

    (Note: The word *mediator* means *go-between* or *peacemaker*.[5])

Now look back at the picture you drew of Jacob's dream. What do you think is the proper interpretation of what he saw?

33. Jacob responds to what he has seen by setting up a pillar to mark the spot and by taking a vow. What do Jacob's words and actions indicate about the state of his belief? About how he views God?

34. **APPLY:** In what current circumstance have you felt that perhaps God is absent? How is Jacob's vision a vision for you? How should it change the way you pray about that circumstance? The way you react to it?

WRAP-UP

What aspect of God's character has this week's passage of Genesis shown you more clearly?

Fill in the following statement:
Knowing that God is _____ shows me that I am _____.
What one step can you take this week to better live in light of this truth?

INTRODUCTORY QUESTION: Where are you in the birth order of your siblings? What role has your place in the family played in the development of your personality?

1. OBSERVE: (question 11, p. 74) The birthright of the firstborn son entitled Esau to a double portion of the inheritance as well as leadership of the family after his father's death.[6] What do you think is meant by the statement, "Thus Esau despised his birthright" (25:34)?

APPLY: (question 13, p. 75) When have you been tempted to give up a long-term gift from God for something that would bring immediate pleasure? Think of an example from your own life.

2. OBSERVE: (question 16, p. 76) Note the similarities in what followed the test of famine for Isaac and for Abraham. How did both experience material blessing, strife, and separation?

APPLY: (question 20, p. 77) Isaac follows the example of his father Abraham, repeating his sin. Who looks to you as a spiritual parent?

How can you model godliness for the person you noted, both in the way you obey and in the way you handle your own mistakes?

3. OBSERVE: (question 25, p. 79) We can assume Rebekah would have told Isaac that God intends the blessing to be given to Jacob (Gen. 25:23). Isaac determines to bless Esau despite most likely knowing that information. Read Galatians 6:7. How did Isaac learn the truth of this verse with regard to practicing deception? (Remember Genesis 26:7.) Practicing favoritism?

APPLY: (question 26, p. 79) How have you learned the truth of Galatians 6:7 in your own life? What seeds of deception or favoritism have yielded a hard harvest within your primary relationships? How have you worked (or how might you work) to sow peace into those relationships?

4. OBSERVE: (question 33, p. 83) Jacob responds to what he has seen by setting up a pillar to mark the spot and by taking a vow. What do Jacob's words and actions indicate about the state of his belief? About how he views God?

APPLY: (question 34, p. 83) In what current circumstance have you felt that perhaps God is absent? How is Jacob's vision a vision for you? How should it change the way you pray about that circumstance? The way you react to it?

5. WRAP-UP: What aspect of God's character has this week's passage of Genesis shown you more clearly?

Fill in the following statement:

Knowing that God is _____ shows me that I am _____.

What one step can you take this week to better live in light of this truth?

WEEK FIVE | VIEWER GUIDE NOTES

Teaching sessions available
for purchase or rent at
LifeWay.com/GodOfCovenant

WEEK FIVE: SIBLING RIVALRY   87

WEEK SIX:

EXILE AND RECONCILIATION

When we left Jacob last week, he was fleeing his brother, whom he had cheated twice through deceit and trickery. On his flight, Jacob received a vision from God, to which he responded with conditional faithfulness. Is there any hope for this guy?

This week we will watch as God works on the heart of Jacob, the deceiver. The tables are about to be turned. Think your in-laws are difficult? Jacob is about to learn the value of a word spoken in truth—the hard way.

DAY ONE

READ CAREFULLY THROUGH GENESIS 29–33. IT MAY TAKE SOME TIME! THEN ANSWER THE QUESTIONS BELOW.

1. Summarize each chapter in one to two sentences:
    CHAPTER 29

    CHAPTER 30

    CHAPTER 31

    CHAPTER 32

    CHAPTER 33

DAY TWO
NOW LOOK AT GENESIS 29–30:24.

2. Compare Jacob's meeting of Rachel (29:1-14) with Abraham's servant's meeting of Rebekah (24:1-33). How are they similar? What differences do you note? List them in the table below:

SIMILARITIES	DIFFERENCES

3. What do you think accounts for Jacob's immediate emotional response upon encountering Rachel (29:9-12)?

4. In 29:21-30, how do we see Jacob, the deceiver, receive a taste of his own medicine? List as many parallels as you can find between Jacob's deceptive practices and Laban's.

5. How does God compensate Leah for being rejected by her husband (29:31)?

6. How does Jacob's response to Rachel's barrenness (30:2) compare to his father Isaac's response to the same problem (25:21)?

7. As with Sarai's servant Hagar, custom allowed for children born of a wife's servant to be legally adopted by the wife. In the table below, note the names of each wife's children. If the child was born of one of her servants, note the servant's name in parentheses to the side. Note also the meaning signified by each child's name (use the footnotes in your Bible).

CHILDREN OF LEAH		CHILDREN OF RACHEL	
NAME	MEANING	NAME	MEANING

8. Who was the clear winner in this contest for offspring?

Do you think she felt like the winner? Why or why not?

9. **APPLY:** When have you striven to win the approval or affection of someone? What did you learn from that experience? Give Leah the best advice you can think of in the space below.

NOW LOOK AT GENESIS 30:25-43

10. In 30:27, we learn the reason for Jacob's success as a herdsman for Laban. What is it?

    What is Laban unwilling to grant because of this (30:25)?

11. In 30:31-33, what business proposition does Jacob make? Write it in your own words below.

12. Note in 30:33 what character trait Jacob says "will answer for [him] later": _____. What does this tell you about Jacob after fourteen years in the service of his father-in-law?

13. In 30:34-36, how does Laban attempt to cheat Jacob once again?

14. Common belief among herdsmen of the time held that whatever images an animal saw while in the act of mating would affect its offspring.[1] Do you think Jacob's spotted and speckled sticks (30:37-43) were the reason for his success with the flock? Why or why not?

15. **APPLY:** What temptation do we face any time our own efforts play a role in God-ordained success? Think of an example from your own life and note it below. What is the right way to regard personal success?

NOW LOOK AT CHAPTER 31.

16. What causes Jacob to leave for home?

17. In 31:12, what does Jacob learn about his spotted and speckled sticks?

18. In 31:13, of what location is Jacob reminded?

19. In 31:14-16, what do Rachel and Leah acknowledge about their father?

20. Why do you think Rachel stole her father's household gods (31:19)? List some possibilities below.

21. Which of the following best describes Laban's words in 31:25-30?

_____ The heartfelt sorrow of a wounded parent

_____ A manipulative rant

_____ Other: _____

22. How does Jacob answer Laban (31:31-32,36-42)?

_____ With deceit
_____ With humor
_____ With honesty

How is this noteworthy?

23. How does Rachel avoid having her saddle searched (31:35)?

24. In 31:43, in a brief moment of honesty, what does Laban reveal that he believes?

25. On what terms do Jacob and Laban part? Does Laban's covenant sound more like a promise or a threat?

26. **APPLY:** The story of Jacob and Laban illustrates that there are some people with whom it is virtually impossible to reconcile. How should we, as believers, deal with such people? Cite any Scripture that supports your answer.

DAY FIVE
NOW LOOK AT GENESIS CHAPTER 32.

27. As Jacob goes to face his brother, what reassurance does he get (32:1)?

28. What does Jacob assume in 32:6-8? What is his emotional response?

29. What is Jacob's next response (32:9-12)? How is it significant?

30. In 32:13-21, what is Jacob's strategy for meeting Esau? Describe it briefly.

31. In 32:22-32, we have a story as bizarre as any we have read so far. We will discuss it in our time together, but for now, note the following:

    Why do you think the "man" asks Jacob what his name is?

    What is the new name given to Jacob?

In the original language, the name means *he strives with God* or *God strives*.

In what ways has God striven with Jacob?

Why do you think the "man" does not give his own name?

32. **APPLY:** What fear or doubt has caused you to "wrestle with God"? Have you seen an outcome similar to the one Jacob experienced? What has God taught you through your times of wrestling?

NOW LOOK AT GENESIS 33.

33. What surprise ending do we find?

34. How are Jacob/Israel's words in 33:11 fitting, given his history with his brother?

35. Jacob/Israel builds an altar in Shechem, as his grandfather Abraham did before him. What is the meaning of the name he gives to the place?

What does this tell you about Jacob the deceiver, now Israel? Who does he finally know has given him the blessing and the birthright?

WRAP-UP

What aspect of God's character has this week's passage of Genesis shown you more clearly?

Fill in the following statement:
Knowing that God is _____ shows me that I am
_____.
What one step can you take this week to better live in light of this truth?

WEEK SIX | GROUP DISCUSSION

INTRODUCTORY QUESTION: What friendly competition do you and your family most often participate in?

1. OBSERVE: (question 8, p. 93) Who was the clear winner in the contest for offspring between Rachel and Leah?

   APPLY: (question 9, p. 93) When have you striven to win the approval or affection of someone? What did you learn from that experience? Give Leah the best advice you can think of.

2. OBSERVE: (question 14, p. 95) Common belief among herdsman of the time held that whatever images an animal saw while in the act of mating would affect its offspring.[2] Do you think Jacob's spotted and speckled sticks (30:37-43) were the reason for his success with the flock? Why or why not?

   APPLY: (question 15, p. 95) What temptation do we face any time our own efforts play a role in God-ordained success? What is the right way to regard personal success?

3. OBSERVE: (question 25, p. 97) On what terms do Jacob and Laban part? Does Laban's covenant sound more like a promise or a threat?

   APPLY: (question 26, p. 97) The story of Jacob and Laban illustrates that there are some people with whom it is virtually impossible to reconcile. How should we, as believers, deal with such people? Cite any Scripture that supports your answer.

4. **OBSERVE:** (question 31, p. 98) In 32:22-32, we have a story as bizarre as any we have read so far. We will discuss it in our time together, but for now, note the following:

Why do you think the "man" asks Jacob what his name is?

What is the new name given to Jacob?

APPLY: (question 32, p. 99) What fear or doubt has caused you to "wrestle with God"? Have you seen an outcome similar to the one Jacob experienced? What has God taught you through your times of wrestling?

5. **WRAP-UP:** What aspect of God's character has this week's passage of Genesis shown you more clearly?

Fill in the following statement:

Knowing that God is _____ shows me that I am _____.

What one step can you take this week to better live in light of this truth?

WEEK SIX | VIEWER GUIDE NOTES

Teaching sessions available
for purchase or rent at
LifeWay.com/GodOfCovenant

WEEK SIX: EXILE AND RECONCILIATION   105

WEEK SEVEN:

TROUBLE AT SHECHEM

At the end of our last lesson, we saw Jacob, the deceiver—renamed Israel—repentant at last. Nearly twenty years in Haran had taught him some lessons about how to live life. Reconciled to his brother, Jacob/Israel had settled down in Succoth long enough to build a house and engage in trade (33:17). The end of chapter 33 found him settled in close proximity to Shechem with his two wives, two concubines, eleven sons, and his daughter.

Perhaps all would be well for Jacob, now Israel. But perhaps he has still more to learn.

**READ CAREFULLY THROUGH GENESIS 34–36, AND
THEN ANSWER THE QUESTIONS BELOW.**

1. Summarize each chapter in one to two sentences:

   CHAPTER 34

   CHAPTER 35

   CHAPTER 36

2. Compare God's command in 31:13 to Jacob's actions in 33:18-19. Where do you think Jacob should have gone after his reconciliation with Esau?

3. Read 33:18 in the ESV and NIV. Note below how each version describes where he set up camp.

   ESV: " … and he camped _____ _____

   _____."

   NIV: " … and camped within _____ of

   _____ _____."

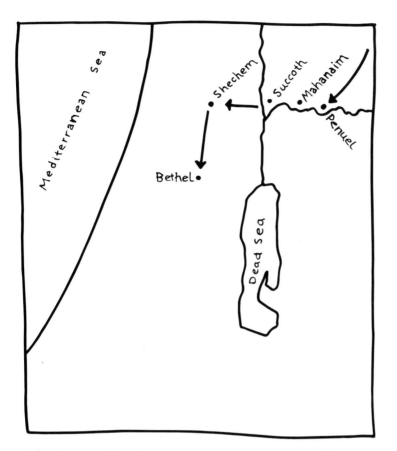

Why do you think Jacob set up camp where he did? Write your answer, and then look back at Genesis 13:12 to see a similar occasion.

NOW LOOK MORE CLOSELY AT GENESIS 34.

4. What happens to Dinah in 34:1-4?

5. Dinah has eleven protective brothers and a large family. What seems to have been true about her excursion "to see the women of the land" in order for her to have been taken advantage of in such a way?

6. Who behaves badly in chapter 34? Fill in the chart below with the crimes each character should be charged with. Note what you suspect their motives were.

	CRIME(S)	MOTIVE
Jacob		
Shechem		
Hamor		
Simeon and Levi		

7. Was the proposal of marriage to Dinah a workable solution to the crisis? Why or why not? Give your best answer.

8. What might Jacob have done or said to bring about a peaceful resolution to the conflict instead of what happened?

9. How was the sacred sign of circumcision profaned (used in a wrong way) by Simeon and Levi? By the Shechemites?

10. How does Jacob's response to the disastrous outcome in 34:30 reveal a serious lapse in character? (Hint: Note all the personal pronouns I/me/my/mine.)

11. Favoritism and deception have wreaked havoc in Jacob's family his entire life. What role does each play in the story of the ravishing of Dinah?
    29:33-34; 31:21

    34:13

12. The last verse of chapter 33 and the first verse of chapter 35 both mention God. How many times does the word *God* occur in chapter 34?

_____

How is this significant?

13. Why do you think this story was included in the Book of Genesis? What should we learn from it about Jacob?

14. **APPLY:** What should we learn from this story about ourselves? Have you ever known you should "go to Bethel" but taken a detour instead? Give an example of a time. What did you learn?

NOW LOOK AT CHAPTER 35:1-4.

15. In verse 1, Jacob is told to "Arise, go ..." for the third time in the record of his life. Look at each of the other two occurrences of the command. Note who spoke them and for what purpose.
    27:43

    28:2

    What does the narrator want to communicate by using the same language in 35:1? In 35:3?

16. Compare 35:1,3 to Genesis 12:1,4. Who is Jacob beginning to become more like?

17. In 35:2, what surprising items do we find have been tucked away in the luggage of Jacob's family?

    How long do you think Jacob has known the foreign gods were among his family members?

Why do you think he orders they be disposed of now?

18. What hindsight does Jacob display in 35:3 in his description of God?

19. In 35:4, Jacob "buried them [the idols] under the oak at Shechem" (NIV). How was his method of disposal and choice of location symbolically appropriate?

20. **APPLY:** God's chosen people carried foreign gods around with them in the land of promise. What about you? What foreign gods from your past do you still hold on to? List them below. Beside each one, write how you might "bury" it with the help of God.

NOW LOOK AT CHAPTER 35:5-29.

21. Why do you think it was necessary for God to cause everyone to be afraid of the sons of Jacob as they journeyed (35:5)?

22. Another burial occurs in 35:8. Who is it?

    Why do you think God includes this detail in the account?

23. In 35:9-15, we see God reaffirming His faithfulness. Note the three statements that God repeats to Jacob:
    35:10

    35:11

    35:12

    Why would He say these things once again at this particular time?

24. In 35:16-20, we have a third burial. Who is it?

Is there anything ironic about the death of Rachel? (See 30:1.)

Rachel names her second son Ben-oni. What does this name mean?

Jacob gives him a different name. What is it? _____
What does it mean?

Where was Rachel buried? _____
What is this town best known for today?

25. In 35:22, we are given a sidebar about some bad behavior on the part of
    one of Jacob's sons.

    What was the son's name? _____

    Which of Jacob's sons was he? (See 35:23.) _____

    According to cultural practices, the firstborn son would be given
    possession of his father's concubines upon the death of his father.[1]
    What attitude toward his father does Reuben's sinful action imply?

26. At long last, Jacob returns to his father Isaac (35:27). And we encounter
    our fourth and final burial in chapter 35. Why do you think that death
    looms so largely over this particular chapter?

27. Compare the account of Abraham's death to that of Isaac's. Summarize the main points of each passage below, and note the similarities in structure.

DEATH OF ABRAHAM		DEATH OF ISAAC	
25:7		35:28	
25:8-9		35:29	
25:12		36:1	

28. Write an epitaph for Isaac.
    HERE LIES ISAAC,

29. **APPLY:** How does the account of Jacob's family troubles prompt you to interact differently with your own? List two hard family relationships below and how you can contribute to them in life-giving ways.

DAY FIVE
NOW LOOK AT GENESIS 36.

30. Why do you think God records in such detail the descendants of Esau?

31. Where did Esau settle (36:8)? The hill country of _____.

32. Note the progression in the genealogy. For each section, note who is being recorded:

    36:10 "These are the names of _____ _____ ..."
    36:15 "These are the _____ of the _____
        of Esau."
    36:31 "These are the _____ who _____
        in the land of Edom ... "

33. In 36:20-30, Moses lists the sons of Seir the Horite. Read Deuteronomy 2:22, and then check the best description for this section of the genealogy:

    _____ These are a branch of Esau's descendants.
    _____ These are the people who originally lived in the area of Seir, who were defeated by Esau's descendants.

34. Remember that Esau married three wives well before Jacob married his first. For a very long time, how do you think Esau/Edom's family compared in size to Jacob/Israel's family?

35. **APPLY:** Judging by appearances, it often seems that those outside the covenant promises of God are prospering far more than the children of the promise. This was true in Jacob's time, and it is true in ours. Give an example of a person, group, or philosophy which seems to be more prosperous than Christians, Christianity, or the gospel.

Do you think Jacob was concerned about his apparent lack of descendants, power, and possessions? As New Testament believers, should we be? Why or why not?

WRAP-UP

What aspect of God's character has this week's passage of Genesis shown you more clearly?

Fill in the following statement:
Knowing that God is _____ shows me that I am _____.

What one step can you take this week to better live in light of this truth?

WEEK SEVEN | GROUP DISCUSSION

INTRODUCTORY QUESTION: Have you ever had to put your name on a waiting list for anything? What is the longest you have been willing to wait?

1. OBSERVE: (question 12, p. 112) The last verse of chapter 33 and the first verse of chapter 35 both mention God. How many times does the word *God* occur in chapter 34? _____ How is this significant?

APPLY: (question 14, p. 112) Have you ever known you should "go to Bethel" but taken a detour instead? Give an example of a time. What did you learn?

2. OBSERVE: (question 17, p. 113) In 35:2, what surprising items do we find have been tucked away in the luggage of Jacob's family?

APPLY: (question 20, p. 114) God's chosen people carried foreign gods around with them in the land of promise. What foreign gods from your past do you still hold on to? How you might "bury" them with the help of God?

3. OBSERVE: (question 28, p. 117) Write an epitaph for Isaac.

APPLY: (question 29, p. 117) How does the account of Jacob's family troubles prompt you to interact differently with your own? How you can contribute to your own hard family relationships in life-giving ways?

4. OBSERVE: (question 34, p. 118) Remember that Esau married three wives well before Jacob married his first. For a very long time, how do you think Esau/Edom's family compared in size to Jacob/Israel's family?

APPLY: (question 35, p. 119) Judging by appearances, it often seems that those outside the covenant promises of God are prospering far more than the children of the promise. This was true in Jacob's time, and it is true in ours. Give an example of a person, group, or philosophy which seems to be more prosperous than Christians, Christianity, or the gospel.

Do you think Jacob was concerned about his apparent lack of descendants, power, and possessions? As New Testament believers, should we be? Why or why not?

5. WRAP-UP: What aspect of God's character has this week's passage of Genesis shown you more clearly?

Fill in the following statement:

Knowing that God is _____ shows me that I am
_____.

What one step can you take this week to better live in light of this truth?

WEEK SEVEN | VIEWER GUIDE NOTES

Teaching sessions available
for purchase or rent at
LifeWay.com/GodOfCovenant

WEEK SEVEN: TROUBLE AT SHECHEM   123

WEEK EIGHT:

JOSEPH
IN EGYPT

Last week we saw Jacob flounder as head of his family in Shechem but finally return to Bethel having buried his past idols. We said goodbye to Isaac and Rachel, and we saw, at last, the completion of Jacob's family in the birth of Benjamin. And we learned of the great nation that came from Esau's line, just as God had promised.

This week we will turn our attention to Joseph, Jacob/Israel's favorite son. We'll watch once again as sibling rivalry tears apart God's chosen family, and we'll trace God's hand in the life of a faithful servant, a life marked by patient endurance of suffering and loss, ending ultimately in great reward.

READ CAREFULLY THROUGH GENESIS 37–41, AND THEN ANSWER THE QUESTIONS BELOW.

1. Summarize each chapter in one to two sentences:

    CHAPTER 37

    CHAPTER 38

    CHAPTER 39

    CHAPTER 40

    CHAPTER 41

DAY TWO
NOW LOOK MORE CLOSELY AT 37:1-11.

2. How old is Jacob's son Joseph at the beginning of our story (37:2)? _____

3. Why does Jacob love Joseph more than any of his other sons (37:3)?

    What is another likely reason he favors Joseph (29:30; 30:22-24)?

    What is the visible sign that Joseph is his father's favorite son?

4. How do Joseph's brothers react to their father's favoritism (37:4)?

    What emotion did they feel?

    How did their emotion reveal itself in action?

5. What do we learn about Joseph from the fact he tells his dreams to his family in 37:5-11?

How is Jacob's reaction to the dreams different than that of his sons (37:10-11)?

6. **APPLY:** Think of a time you have witnessed envy grow into hatred in a relationship. Based on your experience and your understanding of the gospel, what advice would you give to Joseph's brothers?

NOW LOOK AT 37:12-36.

Joseph's journey to Shechem was about 50 miles. Dothan was about another 13 miles further. It was located along the caravan route traders from the north took to go to Egypt.[1]

7. In 37:18, how do you think Joseph's brothers recognized him from a distance?

   In 37:20, what plan do the brothers concoct?

   Why do you think Reuben steps in and speaks up on Joseph's behalf (37:21-22)?

8. What do the brothers do immediately after throwing Joseph into the pit (37:25a)? What does this tell us about them?

   What is Judah's motive for altering the plan to kill Joseph (37:26-27)? What insight do we gain into his character?

9. What is Reuben's reaction to the news of what his brothers have done (37:29-30)? How does his status as the eldest son affect your understanding of his dismay?

10. **APPLY:** Despite the family dysfunction and dire circumstances it describes, what encouragement can we take from this chapter for our own family situations and circumstances?

NOW LOOK AT GENESIS 38.

It may feel like we are taking a major detour into weirdness with this section, but hang on for a bit. Any time you see Judah mentioned it is a good idea to pay attention.

11. Judah befriends a resident of Adullam named Hirah. While dwelling with him, Judah marries the daughter of a Canaanite named Shua. What is significant about his choice of a bride (38:2)?

12. What are the names of the three sons born of Judah's marriage to Shua's daughter?

    _____ _____ _____

    Who did the eldest son marry?

    What happened to the eldest son?

Upon Er's death without an heir, the custom of levirate marriage became the duty of the brother of the deceased.[2] It was Onan's duty to marry his widowed sister-in-law and conceive children with her so that his brother's inheritance (the double portion of the firstborn) could be passed down to the resulting offspring.[3] The children would be biologically Onan's, but they would be legally tied to his brother Er.[4] Though it seems bizarre to modern ears, it was a widely accepted and recognized practice to Moses' readers and to the people of Judah's time. It was even included in Mosaic law in Deuteronomy 25:5.

13. How might such a custom have protected the interests of:
    THE FAMILY?

    THE WIDOW?

14. Why do you think Onan did not want Tamar to conceive by him? What would he stand to gain if Tamar remained childless?

15. How did God respond to Onan's selfishness (38:10)?

    Why do you think Judah feared Shelah would die if he, too, married Tamar (38:11)?

16. What does Tamar do to teach Judah a lesson?

    Does the narrator express condemnation for Tamar? Why do you think this is so?

17. What is your evaluation of Judah's character after reading this story?

18. Why do you think the midwife ties a scarlet thread around the hand of the baby she believes will be delivered first (38:28)?

What is the name of the twin who is born first (38:29)?

Look at the genealogy found in Matthew 1. Read through the first three verses, and note what you find there. Does this surprise you? Why or why not?

NOW LOOK AT GENESIS 39.

19. Summarize 39:1-6 in your own words.

20. Why does Joseph find favor with Potiphar (39:3)?

21. Like his mother, Joseph is easy on the eyes. What trouble do his looks bring on him in 39:7-18?

22. What is Joseph's motive for refusing the advances of Potiphar's wife (39:9)?

23. What do 39:10 and 39:12 tell you about the intensity of her advances?

24. Where does Joseph end up as a result of being falsely accused (39:20)?

25. What pattern recurs in 39:21-23? How is this significant?

26. **APPLY:** How is Joseph's response to Potiphar's wife an example to us of how to handle temptation? What tempts you "day after day"? What pulls at you? How can you stop your ears from listening to the temptation and flee from it?

DAY FIVE
NOW LOOK AT GENESIS 40.

27. Who are the two prisoners awaiting their sentencing (40:2)?

   In what way is Joseph able to assist them?

28. What does Joseph's statement in 40:8 indicate about his character?

29. Does Joseph accurately interpret the dreams of the two men? What does this prove?

30. Why do you think the cupbearer forgot to honor his promise to mention Joseph to Pharaoh?

NOW LOOK AT GENESIS 41.

31. How long would you estimate Joseph has been imprisoned at this point (39:20, 40:1, 41:1)?

   What finally happens in 41:9-13?

Why do you think God allowed Joseph to sit in prison for such a lengthy time for a crime he did not commit?

32. Is Joseph able to interpret Pharaoh's dream? How?

33. Answer the following questions, to help shape your understanding of the story:

Who gave Pharaoh his dreams? _____

Who gave the interpretation for the dreams? _____

Who will fulfill the dreams? _____

In Egypt, Pharaoh was believed to be a divine being.[5] He was believed to be able to influence other deities through magic to ensure fertile crops, favorable weather, and prosperity.[6] How does his encounter with Joseph challenge this idea?

34. How does Pharaoh respond to Joseph's interpretation and counsel (41:37-39)?

35. Read 41:46. How much time has passed since Joseph was sold into slavery? (Compare 37:2.)

36. What detail do we learn about Joseph's life in 41:50-52?

Below, write the names of Joseph's two sons in order of their birth.
Note the meanings their names imply.

1.

2.

What do Joseph's statements after the birth of each child indicate
about the state of his heart? (Note the subject of each statement.)

37. How do you think Joseph felt to be in a position to provide for so
many (41:56-57)?

38. **APPLY:** At long last, in Joseph we find a character consistently worth
emulating because he is so much like Christ. Write below three
specific ways you would like to become more like Joseph.

1.

2.

3.

WRAP-UP

What aspect of God's character has this week's passage of Genesis shown
you more clearly?

Fill in the following statement:
Knowing that God is _____ shows me that I am
_____.

What one step can you take this week to better live in light of this
truth?

WEEK EIGHT | GROUP DISCUSSION

INTRODUCTORY QUESTION: What is the most memorable dream you have ever had? Or do you have a recurring dream? What happened/happens in your dream?

1. **OBSERVE:** (question 4, p. 127) How do Joseph's brothers react to their father's favoritism (37:4)? What emotion did they feel?

   How did their emotion reveal itself in action?

   APPLY: (question 6, p. 128) Think of a time you have witnessed envy grow into hatred in a relationship. Based on your experience and your understanding of the gospel, what advice would you give to Joseph's brothers?

2. **OBSERVE:** (question 9, p. 130) What is Reuben's reaction to the news of what his brothers have done (37:29-30)? How does his status as the eldest son affect your understanding of his dismay?

   APPLY: (question 10, p. 130) Despite the family dysfunction and dire circumstances it describes, what encouragement can we take from this chapter for our own family situations and circumstances?

3. **OBSERVE:** (question 22, p. 134) What is Joseph's motive for refusing the advances of Potiphar's wife (39:9)?

   APPLY: (question 26, p. 134) How is Joseph's response to Potiphar's wife an example to us of how to handle temptation? What tempts you "day after day"? What pulls at you? How can you stop your ears from listening to the temptation and flee from it?

4. **OBSERVE:** (question 31, p. 136) Why do you think God allowed Joseph to sit in prison for such a lengthy time for a crime he did not commit?

APPLY: (question 38, p. 137) At long last, in Joseph we find a character consistently worth emulating because he is so much like Christ. Name three specific ways you would like to become more like Joseph.

5. **WRAP-UP:** What aspect of God's character has this week's passage of Genesis shown you more clearly?

Fill in the following statement:

Knowing that God is _____ shows me that I am
_____.

What one step can you take this week to better live in light of this truth?

WEEK EIGHT | VIEWER GUIDE NOTES

_____

_____

_____

_____

_____

_____

_____

_____

_____

_____

_____

_____

_____

_____

_____

_____

_____

_____

_____

_____

_____

_____

_____

Teaching sessions available
for purchase or rent at
LifeWay.com/GodOfCovenant

WEEK EIGHT: JOSEPH IN EGYPT   141

WEEK NINE:

JOSEPH
OVER EGYPT

Last week we saw Joseph, the favored son, sold into slavery by his brothers. We watched as he patiently endured trials, fled from temptations, and ultimately rose to great power as a result of God's faithfulness.

This week Joseph's brothers come back on the scene. We'll learn how deep the righteousness of Joseph goes, and we'll see if the hardest of hearts can be changed. We'll also get to gaze on the God who lovingly provides for His children, though sometimes through the most unlikely of means.

READ CAREFULLY THROUGH GENESIS 42–47, AND THEN ANSWER THE QUESTIONS BELOW.

1. Summarize each chapter in one to two sentences:

   CHAPTER 42

   CHAPTER 43

   CHAPTER 44

   CHAPTER 45

   CHAPTER 46

   CHAPTER 47

NOW LOOK BACK AT CHAPTER 42.

2. Read 42:1-5 in the NIV and the ESV. What do you note about Jacob's attitude toward the sons of Leah and his concubines? The son of Rachel?

3. Read 42:6-17 in the NIV and the ESV. How does the NIV enhance your understanding of 42:7?

4. Explain why you think Joseph reacts to his brothers the way he does. Why does he decide to deceive them?

    Why do you think his brothers do not recognize him?

5. Joseph accuses his brothers of being spies who "have come to see the nakedness of the land" (42:9, ESV). How does the NIV clarify the meaning of this phrase?

    What proof do the brothers offer that they are not spies (42:11,13)?

How would the fact that they are all the sons of one man diminish the likelihood they were dangerous? Look up Numbers 13:2 to help with your answer.

6. What plan does Joseph propose to his brothers in 42:18-20?

    What do you think was his motive for devising this plan? What does he hope to accomplish?

7. What is the immediate effect of his words on his brothers (42:21-22)? What insight does this give us (and Joseph) into the current state of their hearts?

8. In 42:24, what emotion do you think causes Joseph to weep?

9. In 42:25-35, why do you think Joseph replaces each man's money in his sack?

10. What do you think of the report the brothers give their father in 42:30-34? How would you characterize it, compared to other reports they have given their father?

11. Jacob responds to the proposed plan to take Benjamin back to Egypt in 42:36. How is his response typical?

   When Reuben offers to stand surety for Benjamin, what is Jacob's response (42:37-38)? What does this tell you about Jacob's feelings toward his firstborn son?

12. **APPLY:** Across several chapters and through a series of tests, God is working reconciliation between the sons of Jacob. How have you personally witnessed God change your heart toward those who have sinned against you? How have you seen Him change the hearts of others against whom you have sinned?

DAY THREE
NOW LOOK AT CHAPTER 43.

13. What causes Jacob to urge his sons to go to Egypt again (43:1-2)?

14. Which brother steps forward to remind Jacob of Joseph's warning?

    What is his assessment of what will happen if they do not go to Egypt (43:8)?

    What does he offer to do (43:8-10)?

    Why do you think his offer is met with acceptance where Reuben's failed?

    What change in character does his offer reveal? How so?

15. In 43:15-25, the brothers arrive at the house of Joseph, wary of how they will be received. Ironically, what do they fear will happen to them (43:18)?

What does Joseph's steward say to reassure the brothers (43:23)?

16. In 43:26-34, we see Joseph greet the brothers and serve them a feast. What significant act occurs in 43:26?

17. Which brother receives special treatment?

Note the following:
JOSEPH'S GREETING TO HIM (43:29)

JOSEPH'S REACTION TO SEEING HIM (43:30-31)

JOSEPH'S TREATMENT OF HIM (43:34)

18. Joseph treats Benjamin with blatant favoritism by giving him a portion five times greater than each of the other brothers. He knows that Benjamin is the favorite of Jacob/Israel and has probably been treated with favoritism his entire life. How might Joseph's display of favoritism have been designed to test his other brothers?

What does their response to his "test" reveal about the changing state of their hearts (43:34b)?

19. **APPLY:** Does God ever test us in this way? Does He conceal His true feelings of compassion and appear to treat us roughly or unfairly? Think of a time when you could not see the compassion of God readily in your circumstances. How did the time of testing reveal the changing state of your heart?

DAY FOUR
NOW LOOK AT GENESIS 44.

20. What is the nature of Joseph's last test for his brothers (44:1-13)?

21. Why does Joseph put the cup in Benjamin's bag? Give your best guess.

22. Note what the brothers say will be a just punishment if the cup is found (44:9). Note how Joseph's steward alters their pronouncement (44:10). What is the key difference?

23. When faced with the horrible possibility that his father's favorite son would become a slave in Egypt, knowing that the responsibility for the loss would lie with him, which brother pleads for Benjamin's life (44:16,18)?

    How is this significant? (Look back at 37:26-27.)

    What alternate solution does Judah offer to satisfy justice (44:32-34)?

24. By offering his own life in place of his brother, of which of his descendants does Judah remind you?

NOW LOOK AT CHAPTER 45.

25. What is Joseph's response to Judah's impassioned plea for Benjamin (45:1-3)?

26. Joseph confesses his identity to his brothers and tells them he holds no ill will toward them. In 45:5,7,8, what idea does he repeat three times to explain his presence in Egypt?

27. Joseph understood that God had "sent [him] before [his brothers] to preserve life" (v. 5). How does this speak to us of Christ?

28. In 45:10-28, Joseph, after being reunited with his brothers, sends them back to Canaan. What plan does he propose for his family?

   In 45:24 what final instruction does Joseph give to his brothers? Why might it have been a wise statement?

How does Jacob respond to the proposed plan (45:28)?

29. **APPLY:** Think about the remarkable transformation of Judah—who sold a brother into slavery, married a Canaanite, chased after prostitutes, and cheated Tamar—that same Judah comes to demonstrate repentance and Christlikeness. What sin in your life have you regarded as a permanent blight on your character? What past or current sin seems insurmountable? How does Judah's story give you hope?

NOW LOOK AT CHAPTER 46.

30. In 46:1-4, what two significant occurrences happen at Beersheba?

31. What reassurances does God give Jacob? Note them below and the reason you think God gives them (think back on Jacob's life and the lives of Isaac and Abraham).

	REASSURANCE	REASON
46:3		
46:4		

32. In 46:8-26, we find the listing of the descendants of Jacob who enter Egypt. Note how the genealogy is organized.

	THE SONS OF ...	TOTAL NUMBER OF PEOPLE
46:8-15		
46:16-18		
46:19-22		
46:23-25		
46:27	Grand total:	

Do you think the list of names totaling seventy is a complete listing? Why or why not? Justify your answer.

33. In 46:28-34, Joseph and his father are tearfully reunited after twenty-two years of separation. Joseph gives specific instructions for the family's interaction with Pharaoh. In 46:33-34, note the following:

Where Joseph intends for the family to live:

What occupation the family is to say they practice:

How the family's occupation is regarded by the Egyptians:

34. Look up the word *abomination* in a dictionary. Write a definition for it below that best fits the way it is used in 46:34.
ABOMINATION:

How might being regarded as an abomination by the Egyptians be a good thing for the fledgling nation of Israel?

NOW LOOK AT CHAPTER 47.

35. What does Jacob's assessment of his life in 47:9 tell you about the state of his heart? Is he truthful?

36. How does the state of Jacob/Israel's family (47:27) compare to the state of the Egyptians over the course of the famine and the years that follow it (47:23-26)?

37. What does Joseph solemnly swear to do for Jacob/Israel in 47:29-31? What hope is contained in this promise?

38. **APPLY:** Jacob and Joseph portray a stark contrast. One wrestled against God's desire to tear sin from his grasp, realizing only when his hair was gray that God had always been with him. The other walked in that knowledge each and every day, no matter how bleak his circumstances. In the space below, note a specific relationship or circumstance in which you want to be less like Jacob, more like Joseph
RELATIONSHIP OR CIRCUMSTANCE:

HOW COULD YOU BE LESS LIKE JACOB?

HOW COULD YOU BE MORE LIKE JOSEPH?

WRAP-UP

What aspect of God's character has this week's passage of Genesis shown you more clearly?

Fill in the following statement:
Knowing that God is _____ shows me that I am
_____.

What one step can you take this week to better live in light of this truth?

WEEK NINE | GROUP DISCUSSION

INTRODUCTORY QUESTION: Share about a time you had to act a part. What was hard or easy about the role?

1. OBSERVE: (question 4, p. 145) Explain why you think Joseph reacts to his brothers the way he does. Why does he decide to deceive them? Why do you think his brothers do not recognize him?

APPLY: (question 12, p. 147) Across several chapters and through a series of tests, God is working reconciliation between the sons of Jacob. How have you personally witnessed God change your heart toward those who have sinned against you? How have you seen Him change the hearts of others against whom you have sinned?

2. OBSERVE: (question 18, p. 149) Joseph treats Benjamin with blatant favoritism by giving him a portion five times greater than each of the other brothers. He knows that Benjamin is the favorite of Jacob/Israel and has probably been treated with favoritism his entire life. How might Joseph's display of favoritism have been designed to test his other brothers?

APPLY: (question 19, p. 150) Does God ever test us in this way? Does He conceal His true feelings of compassion and appear to treat us roughly or unfairly? Think of a time when you could not see the compassion of God readily in your circumstances. How did the time of testing reveal the changing state of your heart?

3. OBSERVE: (question 24, p. 152) By offering his own life in place of his brother, of which of his descendants does Judah remind you?

APPLY: (question 29, p. 153) Judah—who sold a brother into slavery, married a Canaanite, chased after prostitutes, and cheated Tamar—that same Judah now demonstrates repentance and Christlikeness. What sin in your life have you regarded as a permanent blight on your character? What past or current sin seems insurmountable? How does Judah's story give you hope?

4. **OBSERVE:** (question 36, p. 156) How does the state of Jacob/Israel's family (47:27) compare to the state of the Egyptians over the course of the famine and the years that follow it (47:23-26)?

APPLY: (question 38, p. 157) Jacob and Joseph portray a stark contrast. One wrestled against God's desire to tear sin from his grasp, realizing only when his hair was gray that God had always been with him. The other walked in that knowledge each and every day, no matter how bleak his circumstances. In what specific relationship or circumstance do you want to be less like Jacob, more like Joseph? How?

5. **WRAP-UP:** What aspect of God's character has this week's passage of Genesis shown you more clearly?

Fill in the following statement:

Knowing that God is _____ shows me that I am

_____.

What one step can you take this week to better live in light of this truth?

WEEK NINE | VIEWER GUIDE NOTES

Teaching sessions available
for purchase or rent at
LifeWay.com/GodOfCovenant

WEEK NINE: JOSEPH OVER EGYPT   161

WEEK TEN:

THE DEATHS OF JACOB AND JOSEPH

At last we reach the end of "The Book of Beginnings." It's time to say farewell to Jacob and to Joseph too—two very different men. I hope you will savor these final pages of Genesis. We began with "In the beginning, God … " And we find at the end of Genesis not an ending, but rather another beginning: The beginning of the nation of Israel's story in the land of Egypt.

**READ CAREFULLY THROUGH GENESIS 48–50.
THEN ANSWER THE QUESTIONS BELOW.**

1. Summarize each chapter in one to two sentences:
    CHAPTER 48

    CHAPTER 49

    CHAPTER 50

DAY TWO
NOW LOOK BACK AT GENESIS 48.

2. Glance back at 47:28. How old is Jacob in this deathbed scene in
    chapter 48? _____

    How long has he been in Egypt? _____
    How old would that make Joseph? _____
    His two oldest sons (approximately)? _____

3. In 48:3-4, what significant facts does Jacob remind Joseph of before
    bestowing his blessing?
    He received a blessing directly from _____
    _____ at Luz.
    He was promised the land of _____ to be possessed by
    his _____.

4. What does Jacob mean by his statement in verses 5-6?

5. Because Jacob gives this blessing before blessing any of his other sons,
    what can we guess is true about it?

6. Jacob/Israel is old and frail, and his eyesight has grown weak. What is
    he very careful to confirm in 48:8-10?

7. What significant act occurs in 48:12? What does it signify that Joseph understands?

8. Joseph is careful to position his sons with the older on Jacob's right and the younger on Jacob's left. What does Jacob unexpectedly do (48:14)?

    Why do you think he does this?

NOW LOOK AT GENESIS 49.

9. Now that the double portion of the firstborn has been given to the line of Joseph, Jacob bestows blessings on his remaining sons. Are they merely words of blessing? Note what Jacob says in 49:1.

10. In the chart below fill in any adjectives or metaphors used to describe each son in Jacob's prophetic blessing/curse. The first one has been done for you.

NAME	ADJECTIVES/ DESCRIPTORS	METAPHOR (ANIMAL, PLANT, ETC.)
Reuben	Unstable, shall not have preeminence	Water
Simeon and Levi		
Judah		
Zebulun		
Issachar		
Dan		
Gad		
Asher		
Naphtali		
Joseph		
Benjamin		

Which two sons are given the longest prophecies?

11. Read Hebrews 11:21. How do you think Jacob's blessings constituted an act of faith?

12. Next to whom will Jacob be buried (49:31)?

13. Write an epitaph for Jacob/Israel:
HERE LIES JACOB/ISRAEL,

14. Throughout Jacob's life, we watch him struggle with his two identities. Read the following verses, spoken by the prophet Isaiah to the nation that bore the struggler's name. Note what you find.
ISAIAH 27:6

ISAIAH 41:8

ISAIAH 41:14

ISAIAH 42:6-7

Why do you think this is so?

15. **APPLY:** Jacob (and the nation Israel) struggled continuously to acknowledge God as El Shaddai, God Almighty, the Sovereign Lord. What about you? How do you struggle against the sovereignty of God? In what areas do you need to set aside your own agenda and submit to God's?

NOW LOOK AT GENESIS 50.

16. The righteous, unwavering Joseph mourns the loss of a father he no doubt recognized as a man of wavering commitment. Does Jacob's lack of consistent righteousness cause Joseph to diminish any respectful element in the handling of his burial (50:1-14)? How is that instructive for us?

17. The phrase "Like father, like son" could not be more out of place in this story. If we had written Genesis, we would have put Joseph in the line of ancestors that led to Christ. Why do you think God didn't do this?

18. Following the death of their father, Leah's sons face a new wave of fear. What causes them to be afraid (50:15)?

    What steps do they take to protect themselves (50:16-18)?

    What is Joseph's response (50:19-20)?

19. Joseph poses a rhetorical question. Fill in the wording below:

    " ... am I in the _____ of _____?"

What does he mean by this question?

Specifically because Joseph does not seek the place of God, how has he repaid evil? Mark your answer:

_____ With revenge
_____ With justice
_____ With mercy and grace

20. How old did Joseph live to be (50:22)? _____ How does the length of his life compare to those of his father, grandfather, and great grandfather?

21. What does Joseph's dying wish indicate he firmly believed (50:24-25)?

22. Write an epitaph for Joseph. Take your time—he deserves a good one.
    HERE LIES JOSEPH,

IN CONCLUSION.

23. Genesis is "the Book of Beginnings." What has it begun in you? Having studied Genesis, how will you walk away changed?

24. What one image, idea, or story will you remember the most from our study? Why?

25. We have made it our challenge during the course of this study to look for Christ in the words of Moses. Reflect back over the ground we have covered, and note below how we found Him there.

    IN THE STORY OF ABRAHAM (SARAH, LOT, AND HAGAR):

    IN THE STORY OF ISAAC (ISHMAEL, REBEKAH):

    IN THE STORY OF JACOB (ESAU, RACHEL, LEAH):

    IN THE STORY OF JOSEPH:

26. Read Jeremiah 29:13. Have you found it to be true in your study of Genesis?

Close in prayer. Thank God for His steadfast love to you. Thank Him that the design and intent of His love was clearly in place thousands of years before you were born. Bless Him that He has given you ears to hear and eyes to see things that had never revealed themselves to you before in the familiar stories of Genesis. Ask Him to continue to reveal truth to you from His Word.

INTRODUCTORY QUESTION: Share a time when you were the unexpected recipient of a blessing.

1. **APPLY:** (question 15, p. 169) Jacob (and the nation Israel) struggled continuously to acknowledge God as El Shaddai, God Almighty, the Sovereign Lord. What about you? How do you struggle against the sovereignty of God? In what areas do you need to set aside your own agenda and submit to God's?

2. **APPLY:** (question 23, p. 172) Genesis is "the Book of Beginnings." What has it begun in you? Having studied Genesis, how will you walk away changed?

3. **APPLY:** (question 24, p. 172) What one image, idea, or story will you remember the most from our study? Why?

4. **APPLY:** (question 25, p. 172) We have made it our challenge during the course of this study to look for Christ in the words of Moses. Reflect back over the ground we have covered, and note how we found Him there.

   IN THE STORY OF ABRAHAM (SARAH, LOT, AND HAGAR)

   IN THE STORY OF ISAAC (ISHMAEL, REBEKAH)

   IN THE STORY OF JACOB (ESAU, RACHEL, LEAH)

   IN THE STORY OF JOSEPH

_____

_____

_____

_____

_____

_____

_____

_____

_____

_____

_____

_____

_____

_____

_____

_____

_____

_____

_____

_____

_____

_____

_____

WEEK TEN | VIEWER GUIDE NOTES

Teaching sessions available
for purchase or rent at
LifeWay.com/GodOfCovenant

WEEK TEN: THE DEATHS OF JACOB AND JOSEPH   177

WRAP-UP

You've made it! You have walked faithfully through the last thirty-nine chapters of the primeval history of the world. Having spent the last ten weeks digging in the fertile soil that is the "seed plot of the Bible," it's time now to reflect on what seeds we have seen planted there.

Here is an optional wrap-up session to help you process what you've learned and keep the big picture in mind.

READ STRAIGHT THROUGH GENESIS 12–50.

As you read, think back on what you have learned in these newly familiar pages. Answer the following questions.

1. What attribute of God has emerged most clearly as you have studied these chapters?

    How does knowing this truth about Him change the way you see yourself?

    How should knowing this truth change the way you live?

2. How has the Holy Spirit used Genesis 12–50 to convict you of sin? What thoughts, words, or actions has He shown you that need to be redeemed? What do you need to stop doing?

3. How has the Holy Spirit used Genesis 12–50 to train you in righteousness? What disciplines has He given you a desire to pursue? What do you need to start doing?

4. How has the Holy Spirit used Genesis 12–50 to encourage you? What cause to celebrate have these chapters imprinted on your heart?

5. Which familiar story of Genesis 12–50 took on deeper meaning for you? In what way?

6. Which previously unfamiliar story or passage stands out in your mind the most? Why?

7. Where did you see Christ most clearly in the Genesis narrative? (Remember John 5:46-47.)

Close in prayer. Thank God that from the earliest pages of His Word redemption was clearly in His view. Ask Him to give you eyes to see how the words of Genesis inform and enrich the words of the rest of Scripture. Confess your great need of Him, of salvation. Thank Him that provision has been made for your need—not in Abraham, nor Isaac, nor Jacob, nor Joseph, nor in any righteous man, but in the flawless righteousness of the Last Adam, the God-Man Jesus. The serpent's head is crushed indeed—thanks be to God!

SUMMARIES, CHAPTERS 12–50

CHAPTER 12

CHAPTER 13

CHAPTER 14

CHAPTER 15

CHAPTER 16

CHAPTER 17

CHAPTER 18

CHAPTER 19

CHAPTER 20

CHAPTER 21

CHAPTER 22

CHAPTER 23

CHAPTER 24

CHAPTER 25

CHAPTER 26

CHAPTER 27

CHAPTER 28

CHAPTER 29

CHAPTER 30

CHAPTER 31

CHAPTER 32

CHAPTER 33

CHAPTER 34

CHAPTER 35

CHAPTER 36

CHAPTER 37

CHAPTER 38

CHAPTER 39

CHAPTER 40

CHAPTER 41

CHAPTER 42

CHAPTER 43

CHAPTER 44

CHAPTER 45

CHAPTER 46

CHAPTER 47

CHAPTER 48

CHAPTER 49

CHAPTER 50

THE ATTRIBUTES OF GOD

Attentive: God hears and responds to the needs of His children.

Compassionate: God cares for His children and acts on their behalf.

Creator: God made everything. He is uncreated.

Deliverer: God rescues and saves His children.

Eternal: God is not limited by and exists outside of time.

Faithful: God always keeps His promises.

Generous: God gives what is best and beyond what is deserved.

Glorious: God displays His greatness and worth.

Good: God is what is best and gives what is best. He is incapable of doing harm.

Holy: God is perfect, pure, and without sin.

Incomprehensible: God is beyond our understanding. We can comprehend Him in part but not in whole.

Infinite: God has no limits in His person or on His power.

Immutable/ Unchanging: God never changes. He is the same yesterday, today, and tomorrow.

Jealous: God will not share His glory with another. All glory rightfully belongs to Him.

Just: God is fair in all His actions and judgments. He cannot over-punish or under-punish.

Loving: God feels and displays infinite, unconditional affection toward His children. His love for them does not depend on their worth, response, or merit.

Merciful: God does not give His children the punishment they deserve.

Omnipotent/ Almighty: God holds all power. Nothing is too hard for God. What He wills He can accomplish.

Omnipresent: God is fully present everywhere.

Omniscient: God knows everything, past, present, and future—all potential and real outcomes, all things micro and macro.

Patient/Long-suffering: God is untiring and bears with His children.

Provider: God meets the needs of His children.

Refuge: God is a place of safety and protection for His children.

Righteous: God is always good and right.

Self-existent: God depends on nothing and no one to give Him life or existence.

Self-sufficient: God is not vulnerable. He has no needs.

Sovereign: God does everything according to His plan and pleasure. He controls all things.

Transcendent: God is not like humans. He is infinitely higher in being and action.

Truthful: Whatever God speaks or does is truth and reality.

Wrathful: God hates all unrighteousness.

Wise: God knows what is best and acts accordingly. He cannot choose wrongly.

Worthy: God deserves all glory and honor and praise.

ENDNOTES

WEEK FOUR

1. John H. Walton and Victor H. Matthews, *The IVP Bible Background Commentary, Genesis–Deuteronomy* (Downer's Grove, IL: InterVarsity Press, 1997), accessed via MyWsb.com on September 5, 2018.

2. Ibid.

WEEK FIVE

1. Kenneth A. Mathews, *The New American Commentary: Volume 1B— Genesis 11:27–50:26* (Nashville, TN: Broadman & Holman Publishers, 2005), accessed via MyWsb.com on September 5, 2018.

2. Ibid, Walton and Matthews.

3. Ibid, Mathews.

4. *The ESV Study Bible* (Wheaton, IL: Crossway Bibles, 2008).

5. "Definition of Mediator," *Blue Letter Bible*, https://www.blueletterbible. org/lang/lexicon/lexicon. cfm?Strongs=G3316&t=KJV, accessed on September 5, 2018.

6. Ibid, Walton and Matthews.

WEEK SIX

1. Ibid.

2. Ibid.

WEEK SEVEN

1. Ibid, Mathews.

WEEK EIGHT

1. Ibid.

2. Ibid.

3. Ibid, Walton and Matthews.

4. Ibid, *The ESV Study Bible*, p. 116-117.

5. Ibid, Walton and Matthews.

6. Joshua J. Mark, "Definition: Pharaoh Ancient History Encyclopedia," posted on September 2, 2009, accessed on September 10, 2018, at https:// www.ancient.eu/pharaoh/.

SOURCES USED IN THE CREATION OF THIS STUDY

Arthur W. Pink, *Gleanings In Genesis, Volume 2* (Chicago: IL, Moody Bible Institute of Chicago, 1922).

Bill T. Arnold, *Encountering the Book of Genesis* (Grand Rapids, MI: Baker Academic, 1998).

James Montgomery Boice, *Boice Expositional Commentary, Genesis, Volume 2, A New Beginning, Genesis 12–36* (Ada, MI: Baker Books, 1985).

James Montgomery Boice, *Boice Expositional Commentary, Genesis, Volume 3, Living By Faith, Genesis 37–50* (Ada, MI: Baker Books, 1987).

Paul Wright, Ed., *Shepherd's Notes: Genesis* (Nashville, B&H Publishing Group, 1997).

The Navigators, *Genesis, Volume 16 of the Lifechange Series* (Colorado Springs, CO: NavPress Publishing Group, 1987).

IT ALL BEGAN WITH THE WORD

VIDEO-BASED
11-SESSION BIBLE STUDY

GOD OF CREATION

A STUDY OF GENESIS 1-11

JEN WILKIN

The opening chapters of Genesis teach us fundamental truths about God. We watch Him bring light after darkness, order after chaos, and rest after toil—all through the power of His Word.

Over 11 sessions of verse-by-verse study, dive into Genesis 1–11 by following three critical stages of understanding: comprehension, interpretation, and application. Revisit familiar stories and historical figures, challenge your basic knowledge, and discover deeper meanings in the text. As God reveals Himself through Scripture, we can only begin to understand ourselves when we first glimpse the character, attributes, and promises of our Creator.

Bible Study Book   005794449 $13.99
Leader Kit   005794451 $79.99

LifeWay.com/GodofCreation
800.458.2772

LifeWay | **Women**

Pricing and availability subject to change without notice.